The Self-Seeking Journey

Journey

Become a Better Version of Yourself

Felisha Upshaw

Names of persons portrayed in the anecdotes in the book have been changed.

The self-seeking journey: Become a better version of yourself / Felisha Upshaw

ISBN- 13: 978-0-578-46987-4
ISBN-10: 0-578-46987-1

My Time Publishing
Memphis, Tennessee

1. Self-help Reference —Self-Help First Edition

ABOUT THE AUTHOR

Felisha Upshaw, originally from a small town in Mississippi, later moved to Tennessee. She travels the states as her primary career is in transportation. She also writes books that she believes can change lives. Her first book, *College Newbies,* is written for high school students heading into college. This second book particularly focuses on self-improvement. Her life experiences are shared in hopes to help others through similar situations. Aside from writing, she enjoys movies, music, seeing beautiful sites and being in the presence of good people.

Contents

Introduction

∽

The days are long and nights even longer. Sadness, loneliness and unfulfillment is running a marathon on me. I have so much on my mind and not a single person to confide in. Of course, I have family, but family is not always loyal, they will spread your business like a California wild fire. One of them may even throw gasoline on it, making the problem worse. Family don't have receipts to prove what they're spreading is true but it doesn't stop the lies. In addition to that, family won't always understand your situations. Don't get me wrong, I love my family more than I love Michael Ealy facial structure, but I cannot confide in them.

I wish I could call a friend and confide but over the past years, I've learned that I only have one, the others are part of the reason that I have become so isolated. They are the reason that my party days are now lonely, long days of boredom. I no longer want to be in the presence of so-called friends with hidden agendas. No, I'm not mad or holding grudges against anyone, because I haven't always been the perfect friend either but sometimes it's best to move forward in separate directions.

So, family and friends are out. Sure, I can talk to God but when you're in a space with low energy and hopelessness. You're not able to pray for yourself (at least I'm not). All this pain suppresses me and I'm so tired of waking up to the same feelings day after day.

What am I supposed to do?

At one point in my life, long ago, this was my reality and today I see several people going through the same emotions as I did. I think certain emotions keeps us weak because we don't know who we are. I certainly didn't. I struggled with my identity. I didn't know who I was, I didn't know where I was going, I was easily persuaded. I allowed other people the power to tell me who I was and of course that didn't turn out well. The unknown identity was the reason for my sadness. The loneliness came about when I isolated myself. The unfulfillment arrived when I was seeking something greater than myself. Your reasons for feeling down, alone or unfulfilled could differ from mine but my experiences may add value to your situation.

There was a point in my life where I would drink alcohol and lots of it to a point to where I was completely intoxicated, falling out of cars type of intoxicated. I remember sitting in the backseat of my friend car and immediately after stopping, I opened the door and vomited everywhere. I'm almost certain I not only embarrassed myself but my friends as well. What's even crazier than that, me and the crew still decided to party. So, there I was, yuck mouth and all, entering the club.

I didn't even like it, alcohol that is and the after affect (dizziness, headaches, etc.) was more reasons to stop doing it. That was not a lifestyle I wanted for my life or for anybody at that age.

I only did it to remove the thoughts I had about who I was at that time. I would look in the mirror and the reflection was unfamiliar, the struggle of my identity had brought me to a place of disgrace for myself.

However, as I have grown over the years mentally and in age, I recognize who I am, I know what I want and I see the direction that I'm headed. I no longer allow myself to be persuaded by others, unless it's for a good cause. I conquered unfulfillment, sadness, loneliness and every other draining emotion by going through the motions and facing them head-on.

I conquered these things because I began a self-seeking journey which lead me to happiness, fulfillment and the self-awareness I needed. Happy because I was completing projects, free from sour relationships, and I was focused. Fulfilled because I no longer engaged in things hoping to fill an empty space. I engaged because that's what I wanted to do, without reason. I turned everything over to God and he created within me a fresh start and I finally re-connected to the person in the mirror.

The self-seeking journey may become painful, because of the ugly truths we discover about ourselves, but it will be worth the result. I can attest, after getting through these experiences I haven't relapsed into a dark space mentally, physically or spiritually. It doesn't mean that I know what the future holds but right now, I will continue to enjoy my life as I would like the same for others.

Will you be healed from life problems? No, this is not what this book or any other book will do for you. Only Jesus can perform that type of miracle. This book will make you think about your life and see it from different perspectives. It moves you in a direction to be a happier individual. I want you to become addicted to yourself. Not in a way that is displeasing to God or not in a way that is conceited, however in a way that makes you content about the woman or man you are.

Things are much more transparent in life when you recognize the power of knowing who you are or feeling better about the reflection in the mirror.

At the beginning and the end of the day, we have the potential to be genuinely excited and fulfilled people versus the person we show ourselves to be every day. We have potential beyond our own beliefs but because we are not living up to higher standards of our self, we are being cheated out of the things that we can have, people we can meet and most importantly the person we can become.

There are times when we are feeling sad and at our

lowest, the devil prey upon us. He sends all the things we desire like "a man" or "a woman." We know this "demon sent" person is no good for us, however we allow him or her in our life anyway. If that's not bad enough, society bends your ear, saying "you are not good enough." Parents and close friends don't see the world through your eyes. Most people are emotionally unavailable and because of that, an internal war has begun. What happens to our emotions when these scenarios occur? We feel bad. We're allowing mental and physical negativity into our space. We hold everything inside and we get distracted long enough to get comfortable in an unhappy situation.

Our stories won't be the same but at times we share the same emotions. These emotions affect us in many ways. It's time to control these emotions, so you're able to reveal the person God created you to be.

I'm writing this book to help you and others stare these problems in the face. I want to change the perspective people have about themselves. I believe everyone should experience the best version of themselves. Looking within is where the healing begins.

Dear Reader

In life, we tend to want immediate results and answers without going through any processes or test from life. We want to lose weight but don't want to diet and exercise. We want expensive materialistic things but don't want to work for it. We want positive results from books but not willing to be open-minded about information written. It's the introduction (in anything) that lets you know what you're getting into. In saying that, I encourage you to read every section in this book, even the ones you may not find exciting (life is not always exciting). Read the sections that opposes your beliefs. Listen my friend, read everything. You didn't think I'd spend years writing this book only to have you skip sections, did you? I'm hitting you with the nitty gritty, so you can take this baby home and get well acquainted with not only the words throughout these pages but with me as well. My experiences could possibly put a smile on your face. Maybe not today but in the future. I invite you to continue reading.

Aside from that, thank you for taking interest in this

book. My personal advice to you is to study it, the goal is to raise awareness in who you are and hopefully you can find fulfillment in your everyday life.

Lots of times when you read books, there are several things you will miss and each time you read it, you will find new information or something you didn't see before. It's possible to not be at a point to resonate with the book but pick it up later and find it helpful. I've had that experience with certain books in the past.

Steve Harvey's book, *Act like a Success, Think like a Success* was one of them. For a minute, I was upset, thought I'd spent $20 plus tax for nothing but eventually, I loved it. That's why I never leave bad reviews on books. You never know when you're lead to pick it up again. Well, that and the fact that someone has taken time to write thousands of words in attempt to entertain, inform or encourage others. Thumbs up or thumbs down. This is a complex job baby. This book is not for everyone, but I'd be elated if it helps many. Enjoy.

Who are you? Describe yourself.

_____

_____

_____

_____

Self-Reflect

Looking back over my life, I see exactly where I took a wrong turn. I see where I gave too much time to the wrong people. I understand where I needed to keep pushing and I know where I've made good decisions. I haven't always known these things and that's because I was going, going, going like the energizer bunny.

The wrong turn came about when I was driving 18 wheelers in the southeast parts of the states. I was doing great, seeing different sights, making money and more importantly, I loved the job, however, I decided to quit my job and move to Memphis Tn. That's when the gates of hell welcomed me. Lost identity, persuasion from others, lonely nights, sadness, amongst other things. The wrong turn and down spirals continued, as I was being controlled by the love of my life.

Of course, in the beginning, it was fun, every weekend, I was in somebody club or at the latest event. I was always spending time with friends which is part of the reason my love life was falling apart. That was my problem, not my friends but the sad part of it all, those friends were not adding value, and I never stopped to analyze it. Yes, I was young and when you're young, you give yourself excuses to behave a certain way. When you're young, you're told to live wild and free. However, my life was going in a direction of discontentment and as I grew older, I realized the importance of self-reflection. Understanding the areas I needed improvement was necessary.

Self-reflection is turning to the mirror and evaluating who you are and how you behave. Today, I'm more conscious, I often give myself an evaluation such as the following and I'd like to share it with you.

Reflect over your life at the end of each day, week or month. Recall moments where you were "not in a good mood" "worried" or "feeling drained" or anything negative. Write those things down and beside it, start listing things that could have made you feel better or made the situation better or see that situation from another perspective. I call it *keeping tabs*, we must keep tabs on our mental state, our behavior, and overall well-being. It's like stopping a disease before it spreads.

If we don't pay attention to our problems, they begin to pile up, like garbage and at any given moment, all that mess is dumped on us.

Lay down and close your eyes. Imagine seeing yourself (like an outer body experience)- Now what/who do you see? List three things below:

_____

_____

_____

_____

_____

My reflection today reveals a strong woman with a relentless attitude and a believer in Christ. Personally, I see me being molded into the life I want to live, growing mentally, physically and spiritually. I would not have seen these things in the past, instead, I would have seen disappointment and weakness. In this moment of self-reflection, we should be completely honest with ourselves.

Self-reflection is like looking at an old home, it may need improvement. It may need remodeling and sometimes, it's beyond repair and we're forced to bulldoze and rebuild. It just depends on the condition of the home. Same with your life.

We may reflect differently on matters of life but the point is to look within, look around, acknowledge and release things or thoughts that hold you hostage. Think about past situations, those that still have power over your life today.

There are several areas in our life requiring self-reflection, I've mentioned: Life purpose, beliefs and achieving goals below. We are working to become greater individuals, let's reflect to build and heal. You can continue with other areas in your life that needs your attention. Try reaching areas within yourself.

_____

_____

_____

_____

_____

Reflecting on Life Purpose & Beliefs

At some point, we all have stopped and wondered, "What is my purpose in life?" It can be frustrating if you don't know the answer. There will come a time when you're wondering, "why am I here?" or "what am I supposed to be doing?" Taking a day for deep reflection will be healthy and helpful.

Think about your purpose in life and the direction your life is headed. If you're not sure of your purpose, ask these questions. What is that "thing" that drives you? What do you get joy from? What do you do and can't get enough of it? Some people find joy in helping others. You may find purpose in expressing yourself through art, music, or writing. Be mindful, our purpose could simply be exuding joy and spreading that happy spirit among people.

One thing is definite about purpose, unless you get out and start doing things or engage in new activities then you will limit yourself to finding your purpose. An active lifestyle provides an opportunity to realize what your interest are and in return, you will learn what role it plays in your life and how it coincides with your assignment.

My being active and curious led me to my purpose, writing. I've always wanted to write a book and one day I sat in my one bedroom apartment, thought of a topic where I had most knowledge (at that time) and I begin writing. I learned that I loved words, loved how it stimulated my mind and I felt joy creating a gift for others from my past experiences, in hopes that it would help them. My first book, College Newbies was born as a result of my being active and curious, a book that focuses on helping students adapt to their new lifestyle on campus. Now this one, "The Self-Seeking Journey."

Once you discover your purpose, protect it. There are people who will lead you away from your assignment or belittle your purpose. It may not be intentional, but it happens. Let me say this again, protect your purpose. The smallest things can get you distracted, we all know just as we're heading into glory, we stumble upon rocks on our path. I'd like to think, it's just the work of the devil and his workers. Good deeds are getting ready to be done, creativity is about to take its place, your bank account is rising to an overflow, along with so many other things. Then bam! The devil steps in and rants "not on his watch."

How many times greatness was upon you but there was a hold or stumbling block in your path? Do you really believe there will be no resistance in the transition? If you're lucky/blessed, maybe you'll get a green pass.

Let me give you an example of resistance before transition.

At my previous job, my co-worker was preparing for promotion, she was the Olivia Pope in the office and everything she did was beyond perfect. She was always right and cared deeply for the job, I believe her personality was Type A. She believed the job was her calling and her purpose. Honestly, I'd never seen anyone love their job the way she did and that is why she was the chosen one (for promotion). She was preparing for the level-up, the contract was signed, and she accepted the salary promised but before she was able to be moved, the hiring boss was removed from his position. Wait, what? This is the guy who chose her for the position. What's going to happen now?

Where did that leave my co-worker? Well, she was patient and continued her great work ethics but in the middle of it all, a new butthole manager tried to stop her from elevating. Fortunately, he had no power to stop the promotion. HR called and transitioned her into the new position. What's my point? She had obstacles in the way of what she believed to be her purpose but she eventually made it to where she needed to be. She moved into her new office and received her new salary and new title. Eventually, you will discover your purpose. Keep your eyes open, stay prayerful, stay focused and consistent.

Aside from life's purpose, we have beliefs.

Let's think about our beliefs and are we standing by them. I listen to many people say they are believers in God but do you really believe in God or does it sound good? Are you someone who believes in changing the world? What are you doing to bring about that change? Here is why I ask those questions. Your belief may lead you to your purpose. The belief in God and the desire to change the world may lead you to helping others selflessly, you may start a non-profit organization which helps millions of people. Imagine that.

The Wright Brothers believed they could build and fly an airplane, belief confirmed because now huge pieces of aluminum fly above us every day.

What are your beliefs? I believe us humans can program our minds to create the best situations in life. Meaning, if we wanted to lose weight, program the mind to do so. If you wanted to gross $100,000 a year, you can do so. Program the mind to believe there are no boundaries when it comes to achieving.

It is your belief that will get you results, you may not know "how" but the power of your belief to do what you're wanting to achieve (along with action) will make it possible.

Belief gets you started and the actual work completes it.

Limited beliefs destroy the destination (tweet that). Trust yourself and believe in your abilities to make things happen!

Reflecting on Achieving Goals

It's always good to think about our accomplishments because when we achieve goals, we want to achieve more goals. Some people have negative self-talk, saying things such as "I haven't achieved much in my life." I'm sure you have but since it wasn't big enough, you don't think you have.

But why? Is it comparison?

Since others have achieved more than you (in your eyesight) you think less of your accomplishments or could it be that society has deemed *what is* and *what isn't* important. When you're counting your achievements, no matter how big or small, they are still your achievements.

Think about how you were as a baby. You learned to crawl, walk, run, skip and hop. That was a process, one in which we learned and lots of us learned at different times in our life. There are phases in life and you must recognize what phase you're in. It's okay, if what you have accomplished is not big. Whatever you set a goal to do and reach it successfully, then you indeed have achieved it.

List three things you have achieved this month (no matter how big or small)?

_____

_____

_____

_____

_____

Don't be so hard on yourself, if you haven't accomplished what you'd like. Keep grinding and you will master what you're after but until then, take notice to what has already been achieved.

A small goal can be not drinking sodas for two days, later it becomes a big deal because if continued, you will stop drinking sodas for two weeks, two months and later two years. Do you see the progress and how a small goal has increased to a major accomplishment?

We've talked about self-reflecting on life's purpose, beliefs and achieving goals. What other areas in your life requires self-reflection?

Think about where you are in this present moment. Are you in a space of satisfaction? or do you want more from life?

List below five things that you dislike about your current lifestyle? (Reflect before response)

_____

_____

_____

_____

_____

List below five things that could make your life better? (Don't limit yourself)

_____

_____

_____

_____

_____

These are just a few things to start the self-reflecting process, you can think about whatever you like. The key is to at least take time to yourself and ask questions because sometimes a question is more powerful than any statement. We live in a world full of talk and verbal out pour but we rarely get in a quite space and think. When you do this, try focusing more on yourself than others because you will get distracted with other thoughts. The main objective is to self-reflect.

Recognize Problems

To fix an issue, you must first know there is a problem. For example, if you've been driving your vehicle to work and other places, unaware that you have a heavy oil leak, eventually you will blow up the motor. Why? Because you failed to do a pre-diagnostic check. The engine lights don't always warn us and sometimes we ignore them anyway, right?

Just as we perform diagnostic checks on our vehicles, we must do the same in our life. We cannot afford to ignore the problems, they'll only get worse. Just like that vehicle, you must find the root cause of your current emotions and deal with them. You may or may not be able to immediately see it but it's possible to identify it.

Here are things to consider as underlying problems:

Our children: Kids are in school and their behavior is not how you expected it to be. You're doing everything right as a parent but your child still acts out. Maybe your child has a disability and you're worried that they won't fit in or be able to do things other kids are doing. Maybe you're worried about protecting your child from bullies. Could this be a problem for you?

Our partner: Your spouse/significant other is cheating but you're doing everything right. Cooking, cleaning, paying bills, taking care of the lawn, regular sex, spending quality time and conversing. What else is there to do to make them be faithful? This can surely anger anyone.

Our Demons: Pushing away feelings for the same sex will create a spirit of frustration. You don't want to recognize your lust for your friend or give-in to the touchy buddy on the basketball court. After all, you have a significant other at home. I can see how this would be an issue, wanting to express yourself but worried what would your family think, what would the pastor say, the neighbors, your peers? What would the world think of your lustful thoughts? Lustful actions? How will you handle this problem?

Child Support: I've heard horror stories concerning child support. Mainly men speaking about their baby's mother and being ordered to pay child support but unable to see the child. I can imagine how angry that would make anyone who's willing to handle their responsibility.

Our Employer: You're busting your bottom at work. Excelling in every aspect of the job but your work continues to be unappreciated and overlooked. You've worked ten years and still no promotion or hopeful pep talk about future positions. There has been no mention of receiving higher pay. So, what are we doing here? This was definitely a problem for me in the past. My choice of employment has always been important to me. I mean, this is where we spend most of our time, so for me, it needed to add value in my life, somehow. Maybe you feel the same and this is the reason for your underlying problem.

Our Co-Workers: We all know co-workers have the tendency to strike a nerve. They are nosy and love to gossip, the sad part is they don't even know you. I call them trouble makers and which I'd like to think their problem is not having enough business of their own. I understand its human nature to be nosy at times, that's fair but for those who live to make others life miserable on the job or attempt to get others fired. Yes, they have issues and need business of their own. The trouble makers come to work just to see whose business they can spread, they have perfect attendance, scared something will happen and they're not there to see it. These trouble makers could be a root cause to your problems.

Social Media: Social media can be a monster to your self-esteem, it can be detrimental to relationships or it can be a resource to network or simply entertainment. Whatever your reason for using these platforms are personal but be mindful how it makes you feel after you've logged off.

Our Reflection: Maybe it's not someone else, maybe it's you. We can become so full of hate from not forgiving those who hurt us. Sadly, we hold on to things that happened years ago and depending on the extremity of it. You have good reason to feel the way you do.

I've been told a story of a young woman who had been raped by a man. I believe I can speak for a good percentage of women when I say, "We are angry for her" I can't imagine how angry I would become and I certainly don't want anyone telling me "get over it." This woman said, 'It was extremely hard to get over something like that.'

Now, for those who have hatred or feelings of revenge to extreme situations such as this. This is your trigger point. This is your root cause for the current emotion, and you're feeling helpless. Yes, someone else caused this pain unto you but you're internally fighting the aftermath.

For others, your situation may not be as severe. You could possibly envy others for things they possess (nice car, beautiful home etc.). Obtaining material things does not determine the quality of your life. If you're not secure, not fulfilled, or lacking a lot in your way of living, of course, the gains of others may bother you (but it shouldn't).

Another word for that is "comparing," you are comparing yourself to other people. You're looking at their happy relationship, their nice car and beautiful house. Some even look at another person's hair, clothes or how attractive they are. You may pay attention to how good other people treat this person and you wish, you would get the same attention. Regardless of how extreme the problem may be. These are situations that people face and it's evident that there is a problem within yourself.

This, my friend, is your trigger point, and you may lack self-love. Understand the power of your being, the mind, the body and spirit.

If you're like me, you've made up stories in your head, stories that you have created based on how someone treats you. For example, if you speak to someone in passing but they didn't speak, you assume they don't like you and that could be far from the truth. True or false, you are sold on the thoughts in your head. My point is we sometimes create problems that doesn't exist.

I remember being at a restaurant and someone who I'd known for years spoke to me. Shockingly, I stared and obviously for too long because right before I could say hello. They walked away. Now, to this day, I believe I was called a bad word and remembered as an unfriendly human being. Truth is, I had hearts in my eyes. Here I sat, up close and personal while my crush waves at me. For me, I dreamed of that day but for them, I was a butthole. So, this is why it's never a good idea to confirm thoughts that we have in our head.

Since we're recognizing problems, we should pay close attention to any emotion we feel. For example, we're thinking we have gained weight because we are eating the wrong foods and drinking sugary drinks. Don't get me wrong, that has a lot to do with it but is it the problem? Probably not, the problem could be stress. Stress may lead to over-eating. Stressing over your spouse's late arrivals home or stressing about not having someone to go home to. You may be stressing about your kid's behavior, the choices they're making or maybe the fact that you're a single parent with more than you can handle. It could be stress from the workplace or a sickness. Let's not forget about one of the most common stressors, financial problems. Stress are possible reasons to your weight gain. Note: Stress may also kill an appetite, be mindful of the underlying problems.

Write five things that could possibly be a problem that causes you to feel the way you do:

_____

_____

_____

_____

_____

Once you have identified those five things, eliminate those that has the least effect on you. There is no time limit on this as we are searching for the root cause and riding of it. So, it may take time or you may know exactly what the problem is. Either way, jot those reasons down on paper or in this book. The big key to it all is recognizing and acknowledging there is a problem. Please don't sweep it under the rug because it will only stay there until you trash it.

Some people have a tight grip on things in their past, things they can't change. If you're one of those people, think about this: there are two holes and you have two seeds. One, you can create new and beautiful flowers, (new experiences, new thoughts, growth) this seed is planted on your property so you're able to water and care for it or you can choose the other seed (old regretful thoughts, painful thoughts, bad experiences) planted in the cemetery where underneath is broken concrete and dead soil that may not grow. Which will you choose? The one that has potential to be successful or the one that is already damaged from the root.

The Message Behind the Problem

Staring at the ceiling, watching the days turn night and night turn days, I remember rolling back and forth in my bed, wondering what's next in life. It seemed as if life was at a standstill, I mean the clock was ticking, people were moving, and physically I was moving. I went to work and came home but aside of work and home, nothing was happening, I didn't have a desire for writing, shopping, or going to concerts. Just nothing! I had the money, time was available to me but there was no fire in my step. All I wanted to do was pig out at fast food restaurants and lay around the house.

I was wondering what had changed to make me feel this way, what made my existence so dull and robotic?

Suddenly, after giving HR my two weeks notice, I felt a shift in my energy. I felt alive again. I even worked the remaining full two weeks. I finally realized why I had loss the desire. I was overworked and underpaid, I was a clerk but not just any clerk. I was the clerk that did so much but with little recognition/appreciation. I know most people feel this way but not everyone does the work, I get it but I showed for work, on time, every day. I worked overtime for several months, covering a shift for employees who had quit. I performed jobs that was outside of my work duties. The list continues but you get the point, every blue moon, they tossed a reward my way which consisted of cold leftovers that everyone had talked over, coughed on and possibly touched. I am not making this stuff up, these are true statements.

I was being mentally drained and dedicated to a job that would replace me within minutes had I made the wrong move. There was no appreciation and the place was infested with crabs in a bucket. They did NOT want to see people elevate (well, most of them, not all). My character was totally different, I wanted to be in an environment where promotion was celebrated and familiar. I wanted to walk through the doors and not dread seeing "certain" people. Most importantly, I did not like the person who I had become, I was complaining, talking about the job outside the job, I snapped at people up who may or may not deserved it. It was just horrible.

I was horrible.

At some point, you just get tired of giving your all into something but unable to receive any benefits. I understand it's a job and my only duty was to work and in return receive a paycheck. Nothing more, nothing less. However, when I thought of the options of the world, I wanted more. I had already seen too much. I knew there was a meaningful job waiting at somebody's place of business or I figured I'd create my own meaningful passion (job) or at least one that paid enough for me to be content. I wanted my cake and I wanted to eat it too as people say but I never understood that line, I mean, the whole point is to get the cake and eat it, right?

Anyway, as I mentioned earlier, we ignore the messages behind our problems.

The message for me was to "get another job." So, I chose to make a move, didn't matter if it was a right or wrong move. I just wanted to quit that job. I prayed about it and I feel like God said, 'How many times do I have to tell you? How many doors and excuses do you need to leave? I'm waiting for you.'

I eventually gave a two-week notice and today, the rest is history. I'm travelling the states and enjoying the decision I've made.

Learn to listen to the message behind your problems, trust me, they are there. We're just so hurt or distracted to a point of not realizing it. Always remember it's the WHY in your CRY.

That is your message.

I believe God will put us through training before he puts us in position. That job was my training. That training kept me from giving in and giving up on my current position. What do I mean, well, when I was re-training to drive the semi, "it was hell!" Everything was going wrong but I kept going and here I am, loving the different aspects and adventures of the job.

It's just like a doctor, why would we allow someone to perform heart surgery but never went through training. It's in our hardest struggles that we gain the greatest blessings. Listen to Joel Embiid when he says "trust the process."

What to do after the message?

Use it to your benefit, your passion may be in your pain. I know it sounds like a cliché but it just might fit your truth.

For example, a drug addict can go through a rough patch and later, go to rehab, get clean and open a center to assist those whom are drug addicts. Those who've attempted suicide may work at centers for suicide victims. They know what to say and are more empathetic than someone who hasn't filled those shoes.

Do you see how that works? Not everyone follows that path but many have and will continue to do so. What problems are you constantly facing?

Let's Pause...

How does any of these things help me find a deeper version of myself? How does it relate to the self-seeking journey? Understanding feelings or repetitive behavior of our unwanted actions, helps us to move forward. My friend, I became restless and hopeless because my previous job made me feel empty and agitated. It was a problem. Now, what is that thing keeps you restless or worried? What is the message behind your problem?

Forcing Friendships

In a world of loneliness, people tend to do things that are degrading and in times of desperation, people rob themselves of dignity.

Not only do people accept being degraded but they get completely out of character in attempt to bond with others. They allow corruptive people into their space, just to have a friend. They try to buy friendships just to have someone around.

My former co-worker, Katrina, would have several parties, providing food and alcohol; the guest could enter and eat free. After the free food and liquor was gone, so were the buddies she thought were friends.

I've seen friendships where someone was called out of their name and belittled to their face. Friends do not look down or talk down on each other, not even in a playful way. Those that do are not friends, they are adult bullies, whom desperately deserves your absence. You got to ask yourself, "Why do I let them treat me this way?" See what thoughts pop-up in your mind.

When you force friendships, you'll get hurt. Why?

Anything that is forced, most likely is not a good match.

It's like squeezing into a small shirt, you can wear it but it won't fit, it's uncomfortable, short and embarrassing. Just as you will be in the end of that friendship. You'll be uncomfortable because that's not your crowd, you'll get the short end because the bond was never mutually desired and you'll become embarrassed after realizing this person wasn't on your team.

There are so many people that don't have a friend and would like one. Young people, older folks and kids, everyone wants someone they can trust and enjoy. There are people who have good hearts that would love to have you in their presence. Don't settle for any random toxic relationship. Toxic people spill over onto you, unbeknownst to you, you have become just as horrible as them. It's like a disease. I don't know about you but if I'm catching anything from others, I want it to be good. Something good like a positive attitude or high energy, wouldn't it be wonderful to meet someone who makes you better as a person. We don't think about it but we're either growing with people or being stagnant with them.

Just remember, forcing relationships will not make it a good relationship. You make real connections with people when you are genuine and being yourself. If you are anyone aside from yourself, you will lose pieces of you along the way. You'll find yourself unhappy because your energy is geared towards trying to do things to be accepted. How tiring do you think that will become? Tiring to them and to you, most people want you to think for yourself and do things your way, after all, that's how we learn from one another. It's called individuality.

If you're weird, so what? You love reading and others think it's boring, so what? You love beer, bars, and parties? Well, good for you.

Like I mentioned in my other book *College Newbies,* you want to be the person who you would like to attract. If you're falsifying who you are just to make a friend, chances are you will bring the wrong people into your life. However, showing others the real you does the opposite; the real you regardless of who you are will always have traits that other people would like.

Example, my friend Melony, is a very kind-hearted person but she has an aggressive personality and at times, talks tough. Personally, I can deal with her. I'm not sensitive and I understand in her snappy responses, she doesn't mean any harm. She is a Virgo and Virgos are crazy, they don't hold back. They think they are right about everything. I hate to admit it but most of the time, they are (at least she is). She is a straightforward person and I like that trait. It's just her personality and I accept that. Now, other people sometimes frown on Melony's personality and those are the people who could not easily connect with her. So, yes you will have things people like about you (your smile, your high energy, positivity) and you will also have things others will not like about you (personality, know-it-alls, judgmental ways).

Sometimes people are not going to like you regardless of who you are, regardless of how good your character may be and regardless of how much money you have. That's the way it is but that's not your problem, it's solely theirs. That's why we are seeking self because eventually, you won't care who accepts you and who doesn't, you were gifted life and free will to live as you want.

The practical way to stop forcing friendships is to befriend those who wants to be around. Get with your family, church members or neighbors and hang out at events of your interest. If you don't have anyone to invite, attend a social gathering, an athletic game or a seminar, a workshop or anything where your potential tribe is located.

Good conversations can be held in store lines, doctor offices, paint classes, or waiting for an oil change. The question is, do you make yourself available or do you fiddle with your phone? Never disregard the places you can meet people.

Once you begin mingling with different people, your conversation topics broaden and you get to see things from others perspective. Your very own presence will be so addictive that you will love yourself more and things you're doing. Don't be surprised if others begin to gravitate towards the new version of you. Decent people love good energy, it's like a breath of fresh air (I know I do). Break the habit of forcing relationships. Be you. Love you.

Note: Not everyone is bad or untrustworthy, but many require close analyzing.

Rejection

I remember in high school hanging with two girls (momentarily), I will call them Susan and Courtney. I never considered them friends but somehow, I ended up in their presence often. One day there was a conversation circulating amongst us, involving us three and a guy. I remember Courtney saying, 'Well, me and Susan are friends but Felisha just tags along.'

Ouch! Well, nobody had to tell me twice. I wanted to abruptly say "Girl, you are not even popular, I don't benefit from your presence and I'm nobody's charity case," but I didn't, I've always been nonchalant. People confuse my smooth manner for weakness, however from that day to this day, I haven't been in her presence. Come to think of it, I don't think we've spoken since that day. Am I mad at her? Of course not, if she ever speaks, I'll do the same. If she talks, I'll talk back. I don't hold grudges and to her defense, we were high school youngsters but little did she know, I was my own person and didn't need a sidekick. I guess you can call that rejection (even though I could have cared less).

I've experienced several rejections from certain peers in high school, but I won't share all those stories (not now anyway) but I will tell you that I'm grateful for those experiences because it could be the reason I don't force friendships today. That and my mother's voice in my head saying, 'You don't have any friends, always remember that.' She means, people will betray you, hurt you, they can't be trusted and things of that nature. Every time she says that, for some reason, I think of the movie Water Boy. My momma said "you're the devil."

Let me tell you my friend. You can't please people, you are who you are and they are who they've shown you they were. Don't ignore it and don't lose your dignity in attempt to gain friendships or join groups. God did not create all human lives for you to set sail on one person. Go out and meet different people and yes it will seem hard with half of the world seeming to function perfectly with only social media as their go-to. Others are skeptical about allowing someone in their space as they've possibly been hurt one too many times. Most people are simply introverts, so they're not keen on forming new relationships. However, there are some good people in your community, your church, and maybe your job.

Rejection happens but never think something is wrong with you because it's not. Rejection happens in more ways than one, unlike the rejection from Susan and Courtney, getting rejected by jobs, loan officers and people I admire; well, that hurts. I have been rejected on several occasions such as these. It's not a good feeling, in fact, it feels horrible. However, life has taught me to never stop going through the cycles. Rejection is something we must face at some point in life. Rejection from people, from opportunities, groups and organizations. It happens, but during those times, I've learned to gain understanding and strength. I would like for you to do the same.

Understanding that everyone is not going to like you and you won't always have common interests with others, every opportunity is not meant for you and maybe you're not a good fit for certain groups or organizations.

Gain strength from being disappointed from the experience and use it as a stepping stone to get better. All rejection is not bad, it feels bad at that moment but it isn't always bad; you can view certain rejections as constructive criticism. It could also be God way of saying, there is a tribe that exceeds those who are rejecting you. You know, God is always showing out and preparing tables before those who mistreated you or felt as if you're weren't good enough. Trust him!

Mentally, I'm using my past rejections for writing this section. I remember applying for a loan so I could purchase a car. Unfortunately, I was rejected, my credit score was not bad, however it wasn't good either because I didn't have anything in my name that was paid in full. Friends, let me tell you, that was a painful rejection because I really wanted that car and I didn't want to ask anyone to co-sign, I knew the importance of credit scores and that asking others for their signature was a big deal. However, I sucked it up and asked a few people and of course, the answer was "no." One of my co-workers said he would co-sign but I knew that would come with a price, a price I was unwilling to pay. What did I do? I paid someone $1,000 to co-sign and that's how I was able to get my first car. Go back in your memory box and recall a time when you've been rejected and later received a better career, a better partner or a better platform.

Maybe you were rejected for the auto loan to purchase that old hooptie but later your credit score sky-rocketed and now you can get a new vehicle. Maybe that man or woman didn't want to date you and now you've found someone better. Hopefully, you can relate somehow and be strengthened by any future rejections.

Handle rejections by moving on and finding better situations, people or opportunities. I know it's easier said than done but just as you walked into that space of rejection, there will await another space you can enter and be accepted. Ask yourself, "How did I handle the last rejection?" "What did I do to make it better?" "The person or group that is rejecting me, can I not find those qualities that had drawn me to them elsewhere?"

Just think J.K Rowling was rejected 12 times before being accepted by a publishing company. Stephanie Lampkin applied for an analytical lead role with

Google. She said they turned her down, what did she do? She created her own successful technical app.

J.K. Rowling was persistent and kept trying until someone said yes. Stephanie Lampkin created her own path. It's not the rejection that can hurt you, it's how you react after being rejected. Neither of these women failed or gave up.

Anything you do in life, you must keep trying, until something works for you. Keep at it, until someone notices or either you are the one who does the accepting or rejecting. Let's not forget, you've probably rejected others as well. So, as I said before, never stop going through the cycles of life.

Be your own company keeper

How often are you alone? Are you comfortable being alone?

Sometimes, it's the company of other people that stops us from seeing the person in the mirror? We are so caught up in spending times with friends and being in the presence of our love partner; we forget to take time for ourselves.

When I was in my early 20s, I was club hopping every weekend hanging in bars, and drinking profusely. During the week, I would hang with co-workers play pool and throw back shots. During that time, I was never alone, I was always with friends or the love of my life.

In those moments, things were good, my relationship was everything I desired, I was active, I was living the good life.

Between working, fun and playtime how does one pay attention to what they want? How is it possible to figure out who you are if you are never reflecting on self or never alone? I never thought about goals. I wasn't steady in jobs because they either closed their doors or I didn't like it and decided to quit. Life was simple for me but the things that are simple are not always good for you.

Thinking back, I wasn't growing mentally, physically or spiritually. I wasn't reading to increase my knowledge, wasn't exercising to improve my health, and I wasn't praying in a faithful manner. Today, I am doing all the above because I am focused on self and improving in all areas of my life. Am I perfect? No, however, I no longer drink alcohol (just whine/margaritas on special occasions). I went back to college and received my degree. I have gotten re-trained in my profession as a professional truck driver and this is my 2nd book. I'm no longer allowing others to consume me. My own company afforded me time to accomplish things.

I've learned to be my own company keeper and honestly, I enjoy being alone. Sometimes people can be too much for me. That doesn't mean I don't want to be around others, it just means I'm content in my own space. I'm the type of person who can live alone, can eat alone, and do other things alone and be okay doing it.

There are those that cannot be alone, they must have friends, family, boyfriend or girlfriend at all times. Being alone scares them but why?

It could be the thought of facing themselves and not being happy with whom they are. Maybe they have lacked loved from their parents; now they seek to receive it from their partner. Perhaps, they grew up in a household with several siblings and being alone is unfamiliar. There could be several reasons but only they would know the answer to that.

Are you one of those people?

I must admit after shutting everyone out and getting out of a relationship, I felt lonely and hopeless but I understood the bigger picture. The bigger picture was to elevate, keep my energy high and focus on the positive things in my life.

My past relationship became detrimental to my future and choosing to move forward, regardless of the painful feelings of loneliness and hopelessness, it was the better decision for me. I was not returning to a chaotic atmosphere. Removing everyone was like going cold-turkey and it hurt. I also think God removed friends he knew I wouldn't remove myself and it was at that point, I wanted a change. I adapted to my situation and fought through the struggle of loneliness.

I dealt with loneliness by staying busy. You can try these things too. Watch your favorite show, doesn't matter if you're binge watching seasons. Don't feel guilty about this, you are going through life motions and healing yourself. Do what it takes in the most effective way but also the most positive way possible.

Go to your favorite store and browse. Back in the day, Best Buy was one of my favorites because I loved electronics, at least until, they started watching me as if I was stealing. I had no plans of buying flat screen televisions, cameras or any other expensive gadgets so, my next option was Lowe's and Sears. Don't ask me why, but yes, I visited those stores multiple times a week. I even started to become crafty and buying items from Lowe's, you never know what boredom and loneliness will produce.

Volunteer at homeless shelters, senior citizen centers or any service to volunteer your time and give back to the community. I volunteered for the TN promise, helping high school students transition into college.

Start a garden or plant flowers.

The point I'm trying to make is keep busy, doesn't matter if you adopt a puppy or cat, our little furry friends always keeps us company and are a joy to have.

Once you become comfortable in your own space and find things that you enjoy. You will never worry about being alone again. Depending on others to keep you company or entertain you will eventually cripple you. Try standing on your own and be okay with it.

Yes, being around others is better sometimes but if you could pass the test of being alone then if ever in that position, you would know how to handle it.

Think about this question, does dining at a restaurant alone make you uncomfortable? You're probably thinking it's no fun, who wants to sit at a table with no one to converse with? Well, it depends on how you look at this situation; the very moment you eat alone, you leave an opportunity open for a potential relationship. If you're with your guy friends or your friend girl, others are less likely to approach you. There is also lots of networking to be done in certain places, however, could you do that if you're always with someone? Probably not.

Be your own company keeper; take yourself to the movies, a nightclub, the bookstore, the gym, or to a bar and grill. I've seen a young lady play pool alone. I thought it was the weirdest thing but I also thought it was amazing to play and not worry what others thought. My co-worker and I questioned if we should ask her to join us for a game but someone else had already stepped in. So, that was a prime example of someone being alone and because of that, she was able to meet new people. Others, including us, wanted to invite her for a game of pool. Those are the type of people who are very comfortable with self and have no problem being alone. It may feel weird at first and extremely difficult to do. The more you do it, the more comfortable you will get and this applies to most things in life.

Again, this isn't a permanent act but being alone for a while helps you grow as a person as it gives you time to self-reflect and improve.

The result is finding out who you are. You may think you know yourself but until you sit and give yourself a Q & A, you won't know.

Prayer

∿

I lived in Memphis for 11 years and for a long while, I was on an emotional roller coaster. The latter days felt like a struggle because I was involved in an unhealthy relationship. I had to constantly argue and explain my every move; it was like clocking in and out for work. Anytime I wasn't home, I must have been out cheating, at least that was the accusation. When I attempted to make new friends, K.J (my so-called love) ruined it. I felt like a prisoner in my own home. There I was in my early twenties, dating someone much older than me, trying to control my every move. It was too much to bear, it was mentally tearing me down. It wasn't always bad, in the beginning, we were a happy couple but it was hell towards the end and all I wanted was to end it. So, in the middle of my identity crisis, I had to deal with an unhealthy relationship.

When I finally gained the strength to start praying, that's what I did and honestly, nothing was happening, the same problems I gave to the Lord were the same problems that kept occurring.

Growing up, my mother took us to church on Sundays, so I was a believer and I had not forgotten how emotionally happy I was in the Holy Ghost. The Bible says: "Train up a child in the way he should go and when he is old, he will not depart from it." (Proverbs 22:6). I wasn't attending church but I started to pray once again.

My faith was available but it wasn't activated. There I was praying and praying and crying while praying, I did this for a while before changes begin to happen. It was only after I received a message from God that my life began to change. How do I know it was from God? Well, I crawled out of the pits of hell and onto flat land and from that day to this day. I haven't fell backwards (at least not that deep).

The message came to me through a big body television set (the older version of TV's). I was watching Ice Cube's *Lottery Ticket* movie and he said, 'The same way you got yourself in that mess, is the same way, you get out.' Those words held true as I felt them immensely. Those words seemed so simple but they carried weight away from my shoulders.

At that moment, I felt and heard the answer that I was desperately seeking. I also noticed that faith without work was dead (as the bible states in James 2:26). It was my turn to follow through with action. I left the relationship mentally before I physically walked away. It was a process and it wasn't easy but because I acknowledged my problems, begin to pray and kept a made-up mind, it was possible. My prayers were answered and over time, life begin to change for the better. God will answer on his time and you will hear him when he does.

Do you believe in praying to the higher power (God)?

I understand everyone won't have the same beliefs and I respect that, for anyone looking to another source of power, parts of this section may not interest you; however, I invite you to read it anyway. Simply because having an open mind to different topics in life is interesting and amazing.

For myself, I'm a believer in God and over time I've created a relationship with him. Does that mean my life is perfect? No, it's far from perfection. Does that mean I get everything I want? Of course not.

I openly admit, I didn't always know how to have that connection with him. There were times in the past, where I would say prayers and talk about God but didn't believe the things I was saying. I didn't know how to apply the word of God to my life. During those times is when I felt empty, it was like no matter what I did, I was not fulfilled. Unfulfillment is an internal issue, I dealt with it by turning to prayer. Honestly, nothing else helped. Absolutely nothing. If you don't believe me, listen to Solange Knowles song – Cranes in the sky she confirms it as do many others. I'm not sure of her results but again, mine was building a relationship with God.

When I reached that point of unfulfillment, I was hanging out with people and going to events and shows but afterwards, I was null and void. I dated a few different people (after my relationship) but I couldn't offer anything, no attention, time or love. So, I retracted from all of that and begin to look inward. Today, it's much different, I feel whole and content. My belief and prayers have gotten me this far, along with the prayers of my mother.

For others, keep in mind to be prayer warriors. God is always there, he places people in your life to support you. He places people in your path to give you a word. Messages are prominent, it's up to us to recognize and accept them.

Many people put aside prayer until bedtime which is okay; however, God wants more of your time. He wants us to talk with him anytime of the day. You don't need a set schedule to speak with God. Others only pray on Sundays and no one is judging you (I'm certainly not) but God wants to hear more from you (and me). Several people call unto his name when they're experiencing hardships and guess what? He will still do works in your life.

Seek to form a relationship with God, act as if he is sitting next to you and don't be uncomfortable doing so. At times, you talk to yourself anyway, right? So, why not speak to him.

Ask God to *guide you in the right direction, to increase your faith, and enter your heart.*

Ask him to *bless you so that you may be a blessing to others.*

Ask him to *rebuke the enemies that speak against you, your family and any goal you're working to achieve.*

He is there!

You must give your undivided attention to things you're praying for; be conscious of what you're saying because sometimes after saying a prayer for so long, we say it without thinking. Why? Because it's a repetition of lines and our brains have programmed them word for word. You want to always be present when talking to God. Feel his presence. It's in that moment when you can become vulnerable and give him your problems, fears, and pains.

We pray and it seems as if things are not happening and it feels as if they will never happen. We get discouraged and lose hope. Let me tell you, my friend; if we got the immediate results we desired, then we would not seek a relationship with him. We'd treat God like a wishing well. I'm sure God would be displeased, just as you are when certain people only call or stop by when they need things. Be mindful in prayer and express yourself to God. He will reveal things to you. You will gain clarity and life becomes easier.

As I said earlier, if you have a belief such as believing in God, you must stand behind that belief. Understand that when you are praying that it's not in vain, God hears you but only he knows what's best for you. Those times when you're unable to pray, he still knows what you're feeling, your tears are not ignored, your pain is not overlooked. Timing may be a reason we receive delayed responses from God. Everything has its unique moment. I'm not a minister but let's think about the story of Job in the bible. Satan wanted to prove Job will curse God. So, the test began and everything was taken from him but Job refused to curse God and received more than before. Our lives are similar to Job, sometimes we are being tested and that test could be during the time you're asking God to help. Again, our prayers are heard and not overlooked.

Imagine marrying the first man or woman you date because meeting someone else is too much work or it takes too long. What have you done? You have rushed into a relationship that is not blessed by God. You missed the opportunity with the next man or woman who would have been a match made perfect. The last man or woman wasn't supposed to be there forever, they were supposed to be a lesson, they were supposed to provide a skill, so you would have been knowledgeable about your God given partner. You would have known how to be patient or how to communicate or anything that adds value to this blessed relationship.

Prayer and patience my friends. We shall overcome obstacles.

Speaking Positive Words

The Bible clearly tells us 'The tongue has the power of life and death' (Proverbs 18:21). Yet, we continue to blurt out everything that comes to mind. It's understood that this is no easy task and we will say things that should not be spoken. We say things such as, "I hate this job" or "I'll never lose weight" or "I'll never get that promotion" or "nobody loves me" and the things we shout could be far from the truth but we've attached negativity to us or our situation by believing these words.

Yes, there are environments and situations that doesn't seem hopeful but we must be mindful that others have made a way out of similar situations and the same can happen for you. Let's try changing how you see things and then have a different thought process about it.

We must practice speaking positive things into our life; whether it's a healthy relationship, financial blessing or simply to have a good day. When you wake in the morning, what is the first thought that comes to your mind? Pay close attention to these thoughts. When you find yourself thinking or even saying, "I don't want to go to work today" or "today is not going to be a good day" or "I hate Mondays." Immediately remove those thoughts. If you've ever heard someone say you should trick your brain; that's exactly what you should do.

It sounds crazy but it works.

Start your mornings by saying, "Today will be an amazing day!" Say it like you mean it. Say it until you believe it. "I can't wait to make it to work, its money season!"

Try thinking of positive and uplifting things to say. I know other matters may fall in the way and these positive words won't always work but they will help for most days.

Once you have trained your mind and begin to speak positive words; they will come natural and you should start to feel better. It doesn't happen instantaneously but eventually things will get better. If you're thinking that's naïve and it won't work. You're already resisting progress. If what you have been doing works for you and you're happy with it. Don't change a thing; however, if you need a change, I would love for you to willingly try something different. It cost nothing to speak positive but you will remain bankrupt with negative words. Just like you study the bible or study for a test, you should study life and then put things to the test. Start speaking those positive words today.

Speak positive words over your children, your parents, your siblings and spouse as well. Regardless of what happens in your life. Look at the bright side of every situation. When your mindset changes, so does situations in your life.

When some people get to work, they tend to say, "I'm tired, I'm ready to go home". If you're one of those people; pause and ask yourself, are you really tired or have you just made a habit to say you're tired and ready to leave? Either way, stay mindful of your spoken words. Remove the draining thoughts and vocabulary and replace it with powerful words. A lifestyle of positivity is like a feel-good drug, people will think you're crazy, literally, but it will just be the happiness that has taken root in your spirit.

Write five things you will say each day to boost your energy:

_____

_____

_____

_____

_____

_____

_____

Distance Yourself

 ⌒つ

I remember a time when I was really low on cash, I was working check to check and I had just been laid off from my job. Times were tough for me, so I called this guy who I thought was a friend of mine and asked him for the smallest favor anyone could ask for; two cheeseburgers from McDonalds, this guy told me he didn't have any money and of course I didn't believe that. I said if I'm hanging around people who can't afford two cheeseburgers then why do I need them in my life?

It sounds harsh I know but let me finish.

This is the same guy whom I asked to fix my flat tire and once again he didn't come through. I had all the tools needed, he only needed to change it. This was very disappointing because this is the same guy who I let in my house, eat my food, sit on my couch, who just made himself comfortable in my house. On top of all that, this dude dropped the #2 in my restroom, I mean, I had to consider him a friend, right?

I noticed that I was always giving and never

receiving. He is one of those people I started feeding with a long handle spoon (real long). I couldn't see myself growing in any type of way mentally, physically or spiritually with him. Space is what was needed for that so-called friendship.

It startles us to speak on putting distance between us and those we've known for several years. Especially, if you're the type of person who always need people around. However, to fully sink into the deeper version of you. It has to be done. I'm not asking you to be alone forever, but self-care is healing.

Not only will you put distance between friends but family and others as well. You're pretty much heading into isolation.

I believe in good and bad spirits. I'm not asking for you to believe in it as well. However, if you think about how you feel before you're around certain people and think about how you feel after seeing them, you begin to realize the good or bad energy each person gives off and of course, we need positive vibes to be encouraged and keep up the momentum.

The negativity does nothing but drain you of all life. That's the reason so many people are stuck in an unfruitful lifestyle for so many years. Negativity, bad spirits, and bad energy equals bitterness, no growth and no vision. I'm sure you can think of one person who is always smiling and in good spirits, while you can also think of someone whose expressing death threats and haven't opened their mouth. Protect your space, be mindful of who you invite in your home, your bed, your car, your life. It all matters. Remove these bad spirited people.

Let's talk about distancing yourself, placing distance between you and others is most effective for single people with no kids. I understand if you're married, have a partner, or kids, this will be challenging but plan to take a few hours out of the day or as many as possible to make this work. For couples, we will just call it, *me-time*. It may sound horrible for me to say distance yourself from your mate and kids but it can be done within reason. Don't abandon them, just make time for yourself.

I had a friend girl to tell me that she is "off limits to her kids" while she uses the bathroom. She takes long baths to relax and think. *This is her me-time.*

While distancing yourself, other people will not understand these changes and if you're not ready to tell them "you're seeking yourself", I suggest you find another answer. Deciding to tell your significant other is your choice, however, if you have a supportive partner, I say be honest. Let them know that you are bettering yourself to improve yourself and the relationship you two have.

If you feel, your partner won't be supportive, then I suggest keeping it to yourself unless your "me time" becomes an issue. The last thing you need is to make your partner feel as if you're spending that time with someone else or neglecting the relationship. We're not creating more problems; we are getting rid of them. Whenever you're unsure about the situation, be honest.

You must be the best judge about informing others or not on your self-seeking journey. That decision is solely up to you as you have an idea of how they will respond. The last thing I need is accusations about me, breaking up your home. So, make a good decision.

Your family and real friends will understand; they will support you and give you space. Besides you're not permanently breaking away (unless they're toxic). On the other hand, fake friends will be selfish; they may not understand your decision in which you don't care because they're likely to be on your list of removals.

What's the purpose of isolating yourself and creating distance between you and everyone?

Well, it forces you to focus more on yourself. Pay attention to what you like and don't like, amongst other things. You will be surprised about the things you don't know about yourself. For all you know, you love yoga, hiking, cooking or teaching. It wasn't until I was alone that things start becoming transparent. My alone time gave me the gift of learning more about myself.

Honestly, isolation hurts. You will cry (at least I did) and you will want to hang with friends and family. That's why it's best to make this transition slowly. Slowly stop answering the phone each time it rings. Slowly stop hanging out every time you're asked. You don't want to go cold turkey in this change (unless you're built like that).

Please know that you're going to hurt some feelings. Again, those who love you, will understand and give you space. It takes a strong person to make it through this stage. On the other hand, those who are in relationships, married or have children, it will be easier because you have someone to talk to and spend time with.

Your time is only given to your mate and children. Well, of course, your parents. Friends must be put to the side. I can't stress how important it is to be by yourself for a while. Whether you are in a relationship or not, spend some time with yourself. The more you do, your life direction and decisions will become clearer.

Name three people who are a part of your life that disturbs your mood.

_____

_____

_____

Okay, now that you know who they are. Write a pros and cons list on each person. If the cons outweigh the pros tremendously, they should be removed from your life. As I said previously, there are a countless number of people on earth to form new relationships.

_____

_____

_____

_____

_____

_____

_____

_____

This doesn't include family, sure we get upset or have disagreements with family, but family is there to stay. That doesn't mean we can't be distant with them. Oprah Winfrey said she has told family, 'I will not allow you to treat me this way' and 'when you get some sense, call me'. I just love her but she is right. She also mentioned, leave them in love and if you do that, they will come back. So, you don't have to leave the situation in rage or fighting matches. Just leave in love.

The Break Away

Now is the time to hop in your air balloon and rise above anything and anyone that stresses you. We talked about slowly distancing yourself. Well, now we have reached a point to completely part ways. We are only letting go of the bad influencers, the negative-don't want you to succeed type, people who constantly disrupt your emotions and anyone else that drains your spirit. No matter how bad it hurts, let go anyway. You never need to be harsh towards anyone when removing people from your life. You don't have to make a public service announcement when you're cutting people from your life, trust me, if you do, it will only create drama. If possible, the break-away is done without creating enemies.

The type of people that should be deleted from your contacts are fake friends. These are the people who does not want you to better your life. They will sabotage you before your eyes and you won't even know it because you felt they were trustworthy. Let me tell you, my friend. Pay close attention to those in your camp.

Now, that you are seeking the person you were created to be.

Now, that your light will shine in any darkness.

Now, that the favor of God is all over you.

You will have haters! They come from under rocks, covered in dirt and ready to get you filthy.

Why? Because they are not secure with themselves. They are not in a place of happiness and sadly, many of them are not looking for happiness. They enjoy causing trouble in the lives of others. Who knows the reason people do the things they do? The fact of the matter is they cannot hold YOU down. When it's your time to move forward, do that.

How do you know these people are not for you?

Observation, whenever you tell a friend about your good news and they get quiet, switch topics or just seems unimpressed. Watch them. Real friends will be happy to discuss your achievements, they will respond with joy and they will not be passive about your accomplishments. Real friends are motivators and encouragers, they will be happy about your success. Whenever you are speaking about starting your own business or improving your career and they find reasons you should not. Watch them.

Phony people are okay with you being stagnant, but you need a supportive circle, those who will help you to the next level. They will be truthful and helpful in the situation. Real friends will give you feedback (it could be constructive criticism) but they won't be a hinderance. Please note, it's not always about reaching the next level, sometimes you just want peaceful associations and you don't have to wonder 'what's their motive?'

Next, if they are too involved in your household business (with your spouse). Watch them. You know the saying "misery loves company" well, so does single people. Single people need company (some, not all) you will not fall into their trap, it's okay to listen to advice but make your own decisions.

One of my favorites, if they see you're smiling and happy, you've declared it will be a good day or week and they try to ruin it. Get away from them, now. That shows that even the smallest things you do will annoy them. Who needs friends like this? No one!

I once knew a woman who intentionally tried to wipe the smile off my face. I would be at work, feeling lifted and sharing my joy about how my writing is getting better and how in tuned I was getting with it. Oh boy, why did I do that? This lady start saying things like "writing must be easy" and "everyone is doing it." Whew honey, talking about the fire that came from my ears.

Obviously, everyone is not doing it, she doesn't have one. Writing is not easy and I was offended by her words. I could have easily responded with sarcasm or an attitude or told her how I felt but her intentions were purely evil, some people won't change. She was the type of woman that would be okay with someone having a bad day because she would have something to gossip about but jealous if you're having a good day because she couldn't spread good news. That's too much like right.

It was obvious what she was doing and get this – she was much older, I expected more of her because of her age. However, some bitter people miss the wisdom and maturity train. I had known her for years, had given her chance after chance but she wasn't for me and these people are not for you. It is true misery loves company but please understand you are not a visitor. Your circle of friends should elevate you, not discourage you and vice versa.

"You are the average of the five people you spend the most time with." Jim Rohn

This quote speaks volumes, I'm sure anyone who has a negative set of friends while being the only positive one can relate. If you're not careful, you'll get sucked into the "no vision network." It's painful when you're wanting to discuss goals or ideas to self-improve but your friends only want to party or lay around the house all day. Don't get me wrong, there is nothing wrong with that, but it has to be a balance in all relationships.

You have friends you should completely remove from your circle:

- The friend that is negative about everything and everyone. In a situation where you may have seen hope, your negative friend finds fault.
- The competitive friend that competes with everything you do. When you say you've been promoted on the job, your competitive friend says, 'Yeah that's cool, I just opened my own business too,' If you buy a Tahoe, they need to get the new Range Rover SUV.
- The jealous friend, the one that doesn't want you to be great. When you get engaged, they say congratulations, but their facial expression says different. They may even bring up your soon-to-be spouse's past, the past they've had before you. They say things such as "are you sure you want to marry him?" or "remember when he cheated on you with big booty Judy?" or "Man, you can't turn a hoe into a house wife."

The con-artist who always swindling you out of money, giving you a sad story but later find themselves in the club with a new outfit and new shoes.

Do you have any of these people in your circle? I'm certain there is more where that comes from. If you stop and pay attention, you would know exactly who needs the ax. It's not rocket science, you already know who is and who is not on your team. You just need to be reminded. Sometimes we fail to see the bad apples because we don't believe our friends can be rotten.

Some people pretend well, you must put aside the love and see them as they are. Love will blind us. Think about this, if you are covered in clothing but underneath are permanent burns and bruises; you can't see them. However, if you're naked, you see everything. Remove your blindfold and see them for what their worth.

Moving forward with dead weight, slows you down and may even keep you from your destination.

How do you break away from people who need the boot?

There are two ways: You can drive 300 miles, hop on a flight and go a few more states over and never speak to them again. Sounds dramatic enough, right? This is familiar to me because I've witnessed someone tell their friend, they were moving to another state but they didn't, they only moved across town. I'm assuming they wanted to end the friendship.

Another way to break away is to be completely honest, lots of people don't have the heart to be this direct. Well, what do I say? Here are a few suggestions: You tell them "I am at a point in my life where I only want to focus on me and my family" or if you're single with kids "I am at a point where I only want to focus on me and my child (ren)" and if you don't have a spouse or any kids; you say "I am at a point where I only want to focus on me"

You owe no one a huge explanation. If you choose the honest route, go easy on them.

The other way is to *stretch the truth.* What do I mean? Well, you have no time to talk, you're either working *extended* hours or helping kids with homework. You are doing laundry, cleaning, alone time with hubby/wife. You are skiing in Santa Barbara. Who knows? Whatever you're doing, it does not involve, answering a phone, house visiting or anything involving these *bad apples* and you. Eventually, they will get the picture and stop contacting you.

Be aware, there are those that will smear your name; they start telling mutual acquaintances (and anyone who will listen) that you are "acting funny" and they may say "I don't mess with them anymore." It's okay, let them talk, they were talking behind your back while you two were friends. Why should things be any different now? When you cut so-called friends loose, they no longer have access to your whereabouts and what you're doing. They can't sabotage your greatness or interfere with your peace of mind. You are focused on self and becoming a better version of self.

Reconnecting

Earlier I said to give yourself time away from people. I said to get away from bad spirited folks who leave you feeling angry. Now that you've removed the bad seeds, now it's time to reconnect. You can't be on Gilligan's Island forever.

Start inviting people in your circle that has your way of thinking. Better yet, invite those who think the opposite as you as well. That should be interesting. You never know who will or will not make your life better. The point is to have a circle that adds value to your life. Whoever you admire or whoever personality you find interesting, these are the type of people to connect with. Personally, I love being around open-minded people, those who want more from life or simply just good-hearted individuals. No one will be perfect but finding those close to your desired crowd is better than the negative Nancy's.

Stop reading for a second. Think about someone who you would love to be around often.

Why do you want to be in the presence of this person?

Do they make you laugh?

Do they motivate you?

What is it? Reconnecting is as important as disconnecting, it would be a sad case to collect junk when you're taking out trash. A good start is going to seminars, bookstores, restaurants, poetry clubs or anywhere to engage with like-minded people (your crowd). You do not want to reconnect to old routines, old habits or old friends (unless they made you better).

Uplifting Crowds:
- They can inspire you to do things you once feared.
- Make you want to be a better person.
- Allow you to be expressive without judgement.
- Allow you to be yourself without judgement.
- Seeing things from different perspectives.
- Honest.

Other Crowds:
- Stagnant lifestyle.
- No ambition.
- Gossip folks.
- Vintage thinking.
- Accepting less.
- Closed mind individuals.

In no way the "other crowds" mentioned above is bad, everyone is different in their own way and whatever a person decides to do in life is their business. However, hopefully you are working to elevate in all areas of your life and your choice of people is in the good crowd section. We are seeking self, so why not reach for your highest version.

No Idling of the Mind /Body

I recall several times where I've wondered off into la la land, thinking about this amazing husband and how great he treats me, the gorgeous home with vaulted ceilings and granite countertops, the meaningful job that I find joy performing every day. I was always interrupted by other thoughts of course but the point is, I wasn't in the present moment. The downside to these fairy tale thoughts were thinking of them too much, so much time passed on a daily basis. Once time is gone, you can't get it back and this is not to say idling the mind is never a good thing but too much of anything is certainly not good.

Idling of the mind and body is the quickest way to throw away hours of your life. If you don't believe me, whenever you catch yourself daydreaming or being idle in movement, make note of how much time passed in that moment. Do this for a while, just to confirm what I've mentioned here is accurate. Either way, be conscious about it.

In an idle state, it seems like we're waiting for

something to happen; instead of making things happen. An idle mind/hand is the devil's workshop. The good part about the workshop is we have keys to enter. If you leave a crack in the door, that's when the devil or others can slip in.

This is what can happen in the idle mind:

- Lustful thoughts
- Thoughts of past pains
- Worrying about the future
- Constant thoughts of boredom
- Daydreaming too much and too long

This is what can happen in a busy (conscious) mind:

- Thinking of ways to invest money for a financial return
- Thinking of ideas to open/sustain your business
- Finding ways to make time for self and family
- Discovering ways to improve oneself
- Anything you create intentionally

When you are aware of what's on your mind, you can control it (to a certain extent). Boredom, for example, if you sit around with no guided thoughts, you'll only think of how bored you are. Who wants to be bored all the time? No one. Prolonged boredom can be stressful for many people.

On the other hand, when you guide your thinking,

to reading a book, exercising, writing, watching a stimulating T.V. show, or engaging in something you love; you will not be as focused on boredom itself. This is not to say you will never be bored but being mindful of your situation, things can get better. You'll be surprised of what you can achieve when you guide your thoughts.

How does an idle mind relate to becoming the best version of yourself? To get the best results in life, you want to be focused and present. Idle minds are not focused on anything. That's called drifting through the days. If you drift too much and too long, you'll look back and wonder, 'where has time gone?' Being present in the moments is what creates progress.

Sexual Pleasures

Sexual pleasures? Wait a minute, why are we talking about sexual pleasures, this book is about seeking self?

Well, the happy moments of life are tied to us and if we're creating memories in the sheets with people who needs the axe; then we'll eventually get disappointed. Constant disappointment and growth doesn't fit in the same category.

Most of the time, there is an emotional connection between people, before and after sexual intercourse. Whenever feelings are involved it coincides with your daily life. How many times have you had sex with someone you care about and it lights up your day? Nothing and no one can bring you down from this high. What happens when someone uses you just for sex? Or at least that's what it feels like. It ruins your mood, makes you feel terrible and feelings of hatred begin to develop towards the user. Do you need these distractions in your life?

If you're single, going without sex is no easy accomplishment, however like anything else, it can be conquered. Sex is a mind thing, yes, your body seems to control you in those moments. When things get heated but no one is around to handle the situation; it can be tough! What is the first thing we do? Yes, you guessed it. We call an ex-boyfriend/girlfriend to fulfill our sexual needs. Well, not everyone, some people have fun toys but that's beside the point.

Let's pause for a minute.

How do you feel after calling an ex to handle business? Does calling your ex make the situation better or worse? If you're like most women, you feel used, even though, you initiated the call. You hate to see them "do their thing" and leave. Of course, you were expecting more, maybe some time and extra kisses. Some men won't even bother to engage in four-play. They just *get it* and *go*. How does that make you feel? Will you do this again? Probably.

The idea is to get away from this reoccurring act. Get away from this temporary pleasure.

Men, when you call your ex for sexual favors, how do you feel afterwards? Many of you are completely satisfied and nothing more is needed but for those who would like a commitment; you want more than sex, maybe to lay and hold your woman. Perhaps, mental stimulation. Unfortunately, you called a woman who is not interested in nothing more than sex. Depending on her character, she may even ask for *money* and leave. *Ouch!* She doesn't want any dealings with you. How does that make you feel? I'd imagine, it's not a good feeling. Don't do this to yourself, you can do better.

Sex was the initial target and for that moment, it was good. At least, I hope it was good. Afterwards, you find yourself sulking in the situation you created. You already knew he/she was an ex for a reason. You two did not work out, otherwise, you would still be together. Most likely, feelings are still there from one of you, which is where the problem appears.

If you are wanting to move to your happy place and become the person you are desiring to be; you cannot double back to old habits and unhealthy people. No, they are not necessarily bad but they are not compatible for you. The best thing to do is move on. I know it's easier said than done but under no circumstances is it okay for you to sleep with your ex. It only makes you feel worse than before. Regardless of whether his or her sex is good, these people are off limits. Who cares if your toes curled? Who cares if you went into seizure mode? Who cares if there was an explosion in the ocean? We must choose self! If you're not good enough to be in a relationship with that person, your sex shouldn't be good enough share with them.

Handling sexual urges while you're single will depend on each person. Many people believe that a person cannot go without sex for years, but it is possible. I must be completely honest and not to air my own laundry, but I've went without sex for years and this is how I know it can be done. I'm in my early thirties, you would think a sister would be *getting it on* somewhere. Now, does anyone want to go this long without having sexual experiences? No. I may be wrong but I'm sure it crosses the minds of nuns as well (no disrespect). It's human nature to want that kind of action in your life.

Again, it depends on the person and if you're one of those individuals that don't believe in *forced celibacy* (want to have sex but can't because you will only do it with someone you're in a relationship with) then it will be hard for you to control the urges; here are some things to do to help your sexual desires, I did say help and not cure:

- Pray about your situation: Ask God to purify your mind, purify your heart and put aside those sexual temptations.
- Don't put yourself in the company of someone whom you could share a sexual experience. Someone whom you're attracted to.
- Always keep yourself busy. An idle mind wonders and it may go straight to sex.
- Masturbation will be the best and main cure. Sure, it's not the same but until you're ready for a relationship, this is how it needs to be. Not to encourage bad behavior but if porn videos could make things better watch them.

These four things will help a lot if you are willing to try them. The point of handling your own sexual needs is to avoid adding unnecessary problems in your life; plus, you don't have to worry about unplanned pregnancy or worry you'll catch a disease.

Now, the self-seeking journey for married people is essential. You have more than self to think about and making yourself better will make the relationship better. It will be difficult to look inward and improve if the home lacks orgasmic experiences. This section exists for that reason. Magic have to be created in the bedroom.

The magic must happen and it must happen everywhere. I'd imagine after being married for long periods of time, things become repetitious. You go in the bedroom as expected and get into the same position while touching his or her body the same as always. If you're really dull, you don't even explore the body, absolutely no multi-tasking skills whatsoever. Ugh, what's the point?

I mean there is no unpredictability at all. It's kind of like Tyler Perry movie 'Good Deeds' where Gabrielle Union (who played his Tyler Perry wife) already knew what position he wanted because that's how he always did it. Now, I'm no sexologist or a therapist of any kind but I can assure you that this is boring.

Let's jump into the sexual pleasures. First of all, you're married and it's totally sinless to role play, spank, bite or get freaky in the privacy of your home. In the bedroom or the kitchen counter top, the shower, the couch, the enclosed pool in your backyard and everywhere else you choose to be creative.

Married couples, do you have rules for sex? Are you still sexually active after years of marriage? I heard through the grapevine that many couples stop engaging in sex, shortly after the commitment. I sure hope not. If this is true for your relationship, Judge Lynn Toler will be awaiting your arrival.

The best rule I foresee is allowing sex to be a priority. You cannot put this off. I encountered a woman who said she and her husband *schedules sex.* I'm thinking "are you serious?" Personally, I'd prefer it to be fun or spontaneous but hey, to each their own, if scheduling sex works for the two of you, please go for it. Sex should also be a natural thing between married couples. He should be able to pull you close whenever he wants (granted, the red dot is inactive). She should be able to *go there* with you without asking, "is now a good time?" While it's understood, there will be times when you're dog tired and sex is just not happening. There may be other times when you just don't want to. We get that, but let's not make it a habit.

Sex is like food in a way, you must have it to maintain. We tend to get frustrated when we've gone a long period without food, correct? Same with sex, you're mad at the world when you're not properly handled within a reasonable time frame. Don't starve your partner, give them a quick snack, preferably a full course meal. Sex well and sex often.

When you are married, you should be learning new tricks and ways to make your spouse sexually satisfied. If by chance, you don't have an idea; watch porn and don't be afraid to do so. Porn is okay if you are not addicted to it.

Pay attention to their body. Don't be lazy. I mean, you're grown, you know what to do, right? Again, I'm not a sex therapist, I'm just saying, to build a stronger bond or to be more exciting in your household, you may want to check your sex life. Make sure the sexual pleasures are being handled and before you get offended and talking back to me through this book, saying "who is she to tell us how to work it or not work it?" I'm simply a young girl with a lot of time on her hands who listens to women and men of all ages talk about their sex life. I listen to gays and straight, so I know a thing or two. I took mental notes from these experienced talkative people (thanks to my previous job). Some of what I've been told is juicy and most of it is common acts but married folks get too comfortable. This is a reminder, sex is important. Get it in when you can! One more thing, when your spouse/partner ask why you're being extra touchy, tell them, you've been reading this book and it reminded you to re-ignite the fire.

Habits can make you or break you

$\sim$

I've always challenged myself to lose weight, so I created my own diet plan. No, it wasn't approved by a nutritionist or a dietician, I wasn't sure if it was healthy or unhealthy. I just believed what I had planned was better than what I had done in the past. So, with my own knowledge, I created a habit, we all know that a habit eventually becomes a lifestyle.

Here is how the habit went down:

- Wake up every day to walk the track, didn't matter if I walked around one time, the point was to make a habit of going until I felt guilty for not going. That worked for me.
- After I conquered that, I included squats and weights daily until it felt natural.
- During all of this, I was keeping in mind that I would change my eating habits. I slowly and consciously stop drinking sodas and replaced with water. Slowly stop eating fast food and begin cooking at home.

I kept this going for months, I was losing weight and my energy level was rising. Things were working and this had become a great habit for me. This lifestyle had created a whole new meaning. I've lost weight and working towards losing lots more. Your habit could be different from mine but imagine what would happen if you created and accomplished your new habit.

Let's talk about bad habits, anything you've done over a long period of time becomes a habit. Habits are hard to break; however, they can be broken. Weeks can pass and you're doing good. Months can pass and you're doing good. Years has passed as well but then ONE DAY you are back to first base; wanting to get into old habits.

What triggered it?

It could be several reasons. Sometimes people are just blindsided with troubles of the world and go back to that familiar place that once felt good. They start to drink, gamble and dabble in old lifestyles that you swore to never see again, the list goes on and on. The last thing you want is to start over, no one wants to dwell in misery and that's exactly what will happen if engaging in bad habits.

When faced with the "urge," immediately think about the consequences. Will your old habits create solutions to your problem or create new problems? Most likely, old habits will create more problems. Let's focus for a moment. Focus on your kids, how badly will they suffer if you double back? Focus on your finances, how will that situation turn-out? Will this old habit place your marriage in jeopardy? How does it affect you and your current situation?

Stop. Think. Decide.

We're going to replace those bad habits with good ones. What is your current daily routine? That routine is your daily habit. For most people, you get up, take care of hygiene, get dressed for work, get breakfast and off to work you go. After work, you stop to grab food (if no one has cooked dinner) and head home. For most, this cycle continues the entire working week.

Now, just as this habit has been created. You want to also create one that ensures your commitment to self-improvement. Good habits can keep you in a good mood, if done correctly. I suggest, whatever your hobbies are, include them in your daily routine. Instead of heading home after work, stop by the gym. Instead of watching television, work on your book. Awake earlier in the morning, to meditate or read. It will be difficult in the beginning but keep at it. Whenever you begin new habits, do not get side-tracked. Set a plan and stick to it. What do I mean? Let's say you decide to go to the gym after work. You wouldn't go back home to change clothes. Instead pack your work-out gear and change when you're at the gym. You're more likely to follow through with the plan. Pay attention to your daily habits.

Balance

Balance, does your life have it? Balance helps smooth stressful areas in your life that you didn't realize was present. Balance is something people don't practice often, myself included. Most people spend lots of time in one area of their life. For many, it's all about work, we know bills needs to be paid, family needs food and money needs to be made. For others, its social media, it has become addictive and consuming. There is an old saying that reads, "too much of anything is bad for you."

Food for instance, we need balanced meals. If we were to only indulge in what we enjoyed the most, such as sweets. How healthy do you think we would be? I'd imagine not healthy at all and same goes for our life.

If we only work and not spend time with family, they will be disappointed which lead to questions, requests for more of your time, and possibly arguments. For example, your children may be disappointed because you never attend parent/teacher meetings or you're never at their sporting events. They see other parents involved with their activities but you're always absent. This can be a problem, their behavior may change, just to get your attention.

Balance allows you to be more productive and transparent. To be more productive in life, we must focus on balance in all areas of our life.

The number one area is to take care of yourself first. Life has its ways of taking our attention away from ourselves and placing it on everyone else. I'm speaking to those of you who focus on your children, parents, friends, spouses, pastors and not give any thought to what you need. You matter. Your health, financial growth, spiritual development and your mental state. It all matters. When you're unable to feed these areas of your life, there will be a disconnect in happiness and fulfillment.

Why? You're not taking care of yourself, your balance is off.

When you're lacking balance in some areas, you're not fully experiencing life. If you're not fully experiencing life, it will be difficult to experience the highest and best version of yourself.

What areas of your life need more attention? Is it family, your health, career, or could you simply use more fun? These are not the only choices you have, of course, there are other options such as spiritual focus, financial and several more.

How to achieve balance in your life? Pencil in hobbies (golf, chess, book club, etc.), play dates with children, or seminars for career insight, date night with the spouse, attend church on Sundays or every other Sunday, take a day or two away from work and lets not forget about a cleaning schedule or whatever area needs your attention. Make arrangements to put more time into the areas that are lacking. Make a mental note and write them down for confirmation to achieve this balance.

Write five things that you will begin to focus on - to gain more balance.

_____

_____

_____

_____

_____

_____

_____

_____

Feeling Sad

Sometimes, we can get buried in our thoughts. There have been plenty of times when I was in great spirits, no issues whatsoever, simply living the good life and boom! Down in the dumps I'd go, without a warning, I would be in my feelings, crying and listening to sad music.

Why do we torture ourselves like that?

We dwell in places that are not healthy. For me, it's my thoughts, worrying about next week and today hasn't even gotten started. My friend said it's just my zodiac sign. It's in a Sagittarius nature to live in the future, according to astrology. Well, even if that's true, I don't like it. I believe it's just a part of life and no one can avoid the emotional rollercoaster.

As humans we're not exempt to go through the cycles of life, the trials and tribulations, some of us go through them more than others but nonetheless we all go through them.

It's like a wave of water that we're constantly swimming through and throughout each repetition of laps (test of life) we get stronger, we gain strength throughout the process. Some of us use that strength to build a lifestyle desired or to fearlessly attack goals. Others get drowned in the tides, unable to survive the lonely hours, cheating spouses, the long-lost identity, the absence of real love or the struggles to lose weight.

We can be so weak at times, we allow so much in our space of happiness. For example, the guy/girl who doesn't want a relationship and suddenly we're sad. No, no, no people, chin up! There are too many beautiful people in the world to be worried about a select few. Ladies and gentlemen, place yourself before a man/woman desiring you as much as you desire them. I understand it's easier said than done but we must push past it.

Happiness is a state of mind and we must stay on the right side of the spectrum. When you stumble into sadness as we all do at times, focus on those feelings and try to understand what placed you in that mood.

Sometimes you get sad because something has happened. Other times, you start feeling down for no reason. At least it seems like no reason, most likely there is an underlying cause such as an old unpleasant memory or something that happened earlier in that day and it just now sunk in.

When unwanted thoughts of bad experiences enter the mind, it can drive us crazy. The thoughts just continue to reoccur. What to do when this happens? Face it, face the problem or address the issue and try to deal with it as best as you can so it can stop getting you down in your spirit.

If what you are going through is difficult and you are unable to face it. Try this: Redirect your thoughts into a place of happiness or a feel-good moment. The purpose is to immediately block these unwanted feelings.

Whenever something you dislike happens or is said to you, trash the moment or those words, immediately. Don't put weight on dead situations or ill words. Our mind wanders a lot, it focuses on whatever you think about the most or experiences we wish to have but if we plant the thoughts we desire in it, we slowly, create new thoughts.

At this present moment, I am not feeling my best but what I have chosen to do is soak in those feelings and write. If you are an artist in any way, choose to create something in those moments of sadness. It is in those moments, we create something that is beneficial to ourselves or others. God gives us all a vision, it's up to us to see it and use it.

Find happiness in the day

$\curlyvee$

Happiness is a feeling, one that many people aspire to have. For several of us, waking up in our right mind, full of energy makes us happy. Watching the sunrise or set gives us a blissful glow, witnessing our favorite sports team win is glorious. So many things put us in a good mood, unfortunately we can't stay happy forever. There are always dark clouds hovering like an alien spaceship, waiting to reveal its ugliness and for that reason, creating happiness in the day is necessary.

Be proactive when it comes to happiness.

It all begins on the inside of our homes. What type of mood does your home possess? Rooms with plenty of light changes the atmosphere inside your home. I'd say start opening the blinds to let natural light shine through. Paint your walls white or any light color, it tends to put people in better moods. Is this proven? Well, I'd like for you to tell me. It has worked for me and a number of people I've surveyed.

Dark colors are just that, dark. Brown or black may

have the same effect as a winter season on a gloomy day. Give your home life with bright colors.

Let me ask, what makes you happy? Name three things that make you happy. Why do they make you happy?

_____

_____

_____

_____

_____

_____

As you awake each morning, place one of those three things in your mind, the idea is to increase your chances of being in a good mood. We set the tone for our day by the thoughts we have, the actions we take and the people we encounter.

During the day, we must be mindful of who is in our space. Just think, do they speak positivity, do they have high energy, a sense of humor or simply someone who doesn't wreck your nerves. Everyone you know are not super human people with extraordinary traits but good company is the key. Who was the last person that had you overjoyed for days? Give that person a call.

Happiness can also be created with positive images, positive speeches and television shows that display things you want. I remember being extremely happy and spiritually fed after watching several episodes of 'The Bible' the feeling was unexplainable. At the time, I was searching for a connection with God. Up to this day, that is one of the most memorable "amazing" feelings of my life.

For you, it could be something different, begin speaking positive affirmations as weird as it may feel, it's needed. You are retraining your mind. We want to release the filth, the negativity, the fights you see on reality T.V. or the news and devour things of your interest. Let's not forget about upbeat music, our favorite songs has it's way of making us feel alive. Find yourself a theme song, 'Sia- the greatest' is one I pull when I need a boost. These things become a lifestyle and that my friend, creates happy days.

If you think about certain extremely successfully people, they speak on being selective in what they feed their mind and I couldn't agree more.

Will everyday be joyous? No. Life is not perfect, but we can make it better with a few small changes. Find happiness in your day by doing more things you love.

Understanding Others / Empathy

We as human are perfectionist, we judge, we point fingers, we talk, we ridicule, we do a lot of things that shouldn't be done. All because we never do anything wrong, right?

When our neighbor is being physically assaulted by their spouse. We, the people, zoom in and analyze the situation and voice what we would and what we wouldn't do. We fail to understand that two people created a bond of love and trust which left the victim mentally damaged and confused. We fail to realize that not everyone is strong enough to immediately walk away from harmful relationships.

When our friends are being faithful to cheaters, our verbal outpour weighs heavy on the situation. "Girl, if I was you, I would leave him" or "Man, there is no way I would allow a woman to dog me like that." We have all the answers or at least we think so. Truth is, we don't know what we would do, if ever caught in the same position.

Another judgmental thing that happens on social

media is this: People get talked about in a negative light for putting their business on Facebook, I hear/see people saying "don't nobody care, so why put your business on FB" but that is the problem, nobody cares. That's probably the reason why it's on FB and not being shared with a trustworthy family member, pastor or friend. Not everyone has a solid person in their corner guiding them or listening to their problems. What else is there to do? Put it on FB where they hope somebody acknowledges their feelings or at least say "I see you" or "It's going to be ok."

Perspective is everything, we need to love each other more, be more understanding. People cry for help well before their tragedy strikes. Let's pay attention and love harder. Learning to understand others, seeing things from their perspective is how we grow. We become empathetic in doing so.

What does being empathetic have to do with seeking self? Empathy is what we need and if we're unable to be this way, why should anyone return that favor? Helping others can boost your mood as well as the person you sympathize with. When you learn to see through the lens of others, you gain a keen perspective on various topics.

You're gaining people skills and knowledge. Who doesn't want that? If we're able to do these things, we benefit as an individual. Aside from that, having compassion and understanding for others allows that good energy to flow back unto you. As long as you're not emptying yourself to fill someone else, you should be good.

Compassion for others can start a love war (people enjoying and leaning on others for empathy and not being judged). We should come together as a community, come together in this world, doesn't matter what skin color you are, we're put here to help one another and if we're not doing that then what are we doing?

Being on Earth is a bit of a battle and we must fight to stay on top of our emotions. The emotions that keeps us in a sunken place, a dark place. I want people to rise above everyday normalcy of burdens, anxiety, depression, rejection or anything else that puts people in a box or in a place of anger, dissatisfaction or a place of unhappiness. I want it to be better, many of us want it to be better. A place of love is a place of peace. A place where there are people willing to help others is a place of unity. Where there is unity resides people overcoming obstacles.

To understand others and have sympathy is to shine light in darkness, you must be that light. Try igniting a fire so big until it spreads throughout the household, the neighborhood, and eventually overflow into the world. For example, my former co-worker and good friend, Paige, once said "she was the light in the household. Living with her sister, nieces and her brother-in-law. She faced the death of her sister Cindy, leaving the family (including herself) in distress. What made it even worse is the timing, late November, around Thanksgiving. After dealing with the heartbreak and helping with the burial of her sister. She tried keeping the family strong by cooking Thanksgiving dinner. A dinner that would not have taken place had she not mustered enough strength to make it happen. After dinner, her brother-in-law and nieces expressed their gratitude for the wonderful act of kindness. Paige was the light in the darkness. She had spread love throughout her household. It's the smallest gestures that makes a world of difference.

The Secret Weapon (The Key)

You are the key to everything. It's like walking up to your house. The door is locked. What do you need to get in? The key. Where is your key? In your pocket or your purse. All you have to do is get it and put it in the door and boom, its magic! Same goes for you. You have the key. You are the key. You just have to use it.

Learn everything you can about the key. What are your strengths?

That's important. Some people are great communicators, others have patience. Are you great at saving money, while others are spending? See how you can be of service to them. They want to save just as you and you could teach on how to save and become financially comfortable. BOOM! You have become of value to them and they can now strengthen their bank accounts.

If you don't like the key you have. Spice it up, change it. Wal-Mart and these lock shops have a kiosk where they design your keys. Make it all pretty. Take your key and add value to yourself, whatever topics you want to know more about, fill yourself with that information. Work on mental growth by researching, reading and listening to coaches in your expertise. Collect the information but always use your own strategy and work because when you steal others ideas, it's like using your neighbors key and their key does not fit your door. It's perfectly designed for them as yours is for you. Make yourself available to the world. Somebody needs you for something.

What do you believe you can achieve?

_____

_____

_____

_____

_____

This was my past belief: To become an author of one book.

Doubt reared its ugly head, while writing my first book but I faced the doubt and gave reason to why I can, instead of giving up and saying "I can't." I knew that I could achieve anything I put thought and action into, it was a matter of getting started, staying consistent and finishing it. I understood myself, I am a relentless woman who believes (if its tangible, I can get it). Does that mean it will be easy? No, not at all.

Words of Encouragement

Under no circumstances are we forced to know exactly who we are, what we want or where we are going. Besides, life wouldn't be so interesting if we had it all figured out. It's the process that makes it all beautiful. Too many people are hard on themselves, they don't give enough credit to themselves and I can understand to a certain extent. When there are too many roadblocks in the way, people tend to quit but you can't quit, find the alternate route.

Just look out into the world, into the communities. At some point, there were several tall trees in a wooded area and someone decided to bulldoze those trees to flatten the land and build on them. There was no way to build while those trees were in the way, so decisions were made, they cleared the land in order to build. Like you, you must remove the clutter and start building.

People don't admit things such as being depressed or being lonely and rejected, etc., it's embarrassing, who wants the world to know these things about us? No one, but guess what, a majority of people in the world has experienced the thing you are hiding. If we can come out of hiding and share stories with others, maybe we can learn to be a shoulder for one another. Learn to move through problems together. There is no need to stay in the dumps, not understanding why life is passing by while nothing is changing or not understanding how you're just existing and not living.

Notes

- To find the best version of yourself, you have to be engaging in life. You cannot sit on the couch and watch television all day, sure you see some entertainment. You see all kinds of informative shows but you can't experience life through the big screen. You can only create fairy tales in your mind after watching T.V. but to find your deeper self; get out and be social (outside of social media) online presence is cool but nothing beats a real human interaction. Engage in different activities, what's going on in your city? You never know where this could lead you. Look at life as one big rat maze, by the way, you're the rat in the maze (calm down, you do know you're not a rat, right?) You're searching for cheese, everybody wants the cheese, whatever your cheese may be. For some people it's money, others it's their identity, for many it's love or self-love. Several different things keep us going. We want the best cheese the maze has to offer. So, let's get it.

- To feel better as a person, we must remove some things and people. Holding on to them keeps us vulnerable. We must re-visit our past hurts and heal those wounds. Our mental state needs clarity and relief. Our hearts need mending. It's time to look at self and our behavior for the betterment of our life.

Highlights

- Don't disregard your feelings to appease someone else.

  Name one person that deserves to be placed on a pedestal (by you) while you take an unfulfilling backseat. I'm not speaking about your children, sometimes they will come first and as parents, you will be placed on hold. I'm talking about the outsiders, our times today, it feels like people are cold-hearted and proud of it. I know you are a people pleaser by nature, but you must make yourself a priority. Stop allowing people to be an inconvenience in your life.

- Dismantle the thoughts of insecurity and build thoughts of belief in yourself.

  Thinking of yourself in a negative way blocks your chances of being your best self. You can't perform in a superb manner with doubts, you will question your every move. You excel when you are sure about your projects. When you love, enjoy or have knowledge about your "thing" whatever it may be, then you shall prosper or at least be confident with any outcome. I want to tell you to speak positively and oversee your thoughts, it may seem shallow to most people but it's necessary. Notice your insecurities and work on making them better. If you're not confident in communicating with others, put in the work to change that narrative, start reading as it increases your vocabulary and stimulates your mind. Talk to yourself, believe it or not, the best conversations you'll have are when you're alone.

- Material things won't replace the battles within. Work on fighting the battle and once you've overcome it, you enjoy the material things, in peace.

- Until you recognize your value, you'll always look for outside validation.

- Stimulate your mind, give care to the body and strengthen them both.

Who are you? Describe yourself.

_____

_____

_____

_____

_____

Acknowledgements

I would like to thank God for placing it upon my heart to write this book. Thanks for helping me choose my words and guiding me through this process. There are many things I could be doing to occupy my time but I've decided to accept the joys and challenges of writing.

Special thanks to my mother, Birdie Upshaw, you have always been my rock and a great supporter. I admire you. I love you.

Shout out to my younger sister, Chantelle Upshaw, for her feedback on this project, your honesty is always appreciated.

My friend, Patricia Martin, you're always uplifting and encouraging me. I'm thankful to be included in your circle.

I'm grateful for my team (editor, formatting crew, cover

designer, beta readers). I couldn't have completed this project without you.

Last but certainly not least, thank you for taking interest in this book. My hope is that you enjoyed it and received value in the process.

www.ingramcontent.com/pod-product-compliance
Lightning Source LLC
Chambersburg PA
CBHW031340040426
42443CB00006B/418